TRADEMARK POWER

ALSO FROM WESTPHALIA PRESS
WESTPHALIAPRESS.ORG

The Idea of the Digital University

Masonic Tombstones and Masonic Secrets

Eight Decades in Syria

Avant-Garde Politician

L'Enfant and the Freemasons

Baronial Bedrooms

Conflicts in Health Policy

Material History and Ritual Objects

Paddle Your Own Canoe

Opportunity and Horatio Alger

Careers in the Face of Challenge

Bookplates of the Kings

Collecting American Presidential Autographs

Misunderstood Children

Original Cables from the Pearl Harbor Attack

Social Satire and the Modern Novel

The Amenities of Book Collecting

The Genius of Freemasonry

A Definitive Commentary on Bookplates

James Martineau and Rebuilding Theology

No Bird Lacks Feathers

Earthworms, Horses, and Living Things

The Man Who Killed President Garfield

Anti-Masonry and the Murder of Morgan

Understanding Art

Homeopathy

Ancient Masonic Mysteries

Collecting Old Books

The Boy Chums Cruising in Florida Waters

The Thomas Starr King Dispute

Ivanhoe Masonic Quartettes

Lariats and Lassos

Mr. Garfield of Ohio

The Wisdom of Thomas Starr King

The French Foreign Legion

War in Syria

Naturism Comes to the United States

New Sources on Women and Freemasonry

Designing, Adapting, Strategizing in Online Education

Gunboat and Gun-runner

Meeting Minutes of Naval Lodge No. 4 F.A.A.M

TRADEMARK POWER

An Expedition Into an Unprobed
and Inviting Wilderness

By Glen Buck

WESTPHALIA PRESS
AN IMPRINT OF POLICY STUDIES ORGANIZATION

WESTPHALIA PRESS
AN IMPRINT OF POLICY STUDIES ORGANIZATION
1527 NEW HAMPSHIRE AVE., NW
WASHINGTON, D.C. 20036
INFO@IPSONET.ORG

ISBN-13: 978-1-63391-211-3
ISBN-10: 1633912116

COVER DESIGN BY JEFFREY BARNES:
JBARNESBOOK.DESIGN

DANIEL GUTIERREZ-SANDOVAL, EXECUTIVE DIRECTOR
PSO AND WESTPHALIA PRESS

UPDATED MATERIAL AND COMMENTS ON THIS EDITION
CAN BE FOUND AT THE WESTPHALIA PRESS WEBSITE:
WWW.WESTPHALIAPRESS.ORG

TRADEMARK POWER

AN EXPEDITION INTO AN UNPROBED AND INVITING WILDERNESS

BY

GLEN BUCK

To

FREDERIC W. GARDNER

who blazed the trail

FOREWORD

Why this ado? Wiseacres everywhere are discoursing sagely concerning the trademark. As though it were a new thing in the world! *The trademark!* It is being served to us with the salad at conference dinners; discussed where directors gather; torn into shreds by the analyzing class publications; profoundly expounded by wrinkled-browed lawyers; advertised to a patient public through gratuitous spaces in the magazines; and abused outrageously by those who protest they love it best.

A revival? Yes. For back in the earliest dawn of civilization the trademark had its inception. It has had a fitful though tenacious life in the affairs of men since first things were made to exchange or sell. But it has been only since the development of advertising to its present hopeful state that it has become a subject for conversation in thundering subway trains and at gentlemanly pink teas.

The trademark is in the atmosphere.

Yet, among all the books in the great American libraries there is not one that attempts to make clear its real purposes and uses in commerce. Many shelves there are that are crowded with volumes which have to do with its legal aspects. But careful search has failed to reveal any comprehensive statement that sets down its philosophy, traces its development, or makes the application to present-day merchandising conditions.

This little book then is a pioneer in a

new field. It is a sincere endeavor to bring about a clearer understanding of a factor that is assuming increasing importance in the activities of the times. And it is sent out to a world of thinking men with the hope that it may do a little share toward the advancement of better conditions in that fascinating development which we call Modern Business.

GLEN BUCK

Chicago,
March, 1916

"In this roaring age of efficiency
we do not long support any
institution that does not set its
claws deep in the common life
and hang on"

—*Robert Louis Stevenson*

TRADEMARK POWER

§ 1

Two men, apparently somebodies in the world of affairs, were leisurely finishing after-luncheon cigars on the observation platform of a train that was bearing down upon the great metropolis at the easy speed of sixty miles an hour.   For some time they had been absorbed in watching the telegraph lines, trees, houses, indeed all the objects of the landscape, move rapidly in, as live things might move, toward the narrowing track and vanish at a point in the distance, as though they had been drawn into some deep funnel.   Like an endless conveyor-belt the cross-bound rails of steel rushed from beneath their feet carrying everything with them. From both sides the brightly colored advertising boards came together and disappeared in thin lines. Trees and buildings lost their shape and the brightest colors faded to soft gray as they receded to that common meeting.

But the advertising signs were increasing in number and now almost fenced the way.

"It is a strange thing," said one of the men after a long silence, "but out of the thousands of advertisements that have passed us, there is only one that I can form any very definite mental picture of, once it is out of sight. And that one seems to be impressed upon my mind vividly for all time. The girl with her feet in wooden shoes and her head hidden in a sun-bonnet, that strenuous maiden who is eternally chasing dirt, I can't get away from. She has an attraction for me that is almost uncanny. I pick her out of a crowd as I would an old friend. And try as I may, I can't think of the girl without thinking of the product she represents, any more than I can think of the product without forming a mental vision of the girl. The two ideas are inseparable in my mind."

"But would not the name serve the purpose quite as well—providing you saw it as often," asked the other.

"No! I am sure it would not! And besides I wouldn't see it often. There is something about a design like that that is tremendously more impressive than any name ever could be. It suggests more. It tells a complete story at a glance. It must be that the mind thinks in pictures, for I find it difficult to visualize a name. But it is easy to visualize an uncomplicated design or form—especially if one sees it often."

"I don't exactly see the advantage," said the skeptical one.

"Just this. All cleaning powders look alike. There are dozens of them. But the manufacturer who succeeds in making his particular powder stand out from all the others with the greatest distinctiveness, will, if other things are equal, get the greater share of the sales. It has just come to me since we have been sitting here that a good trademark is the simplest and most powerful means of clearly separating a product from all others of its kind. It gives something for the memory to hang to."

And there, on that speeding train, as the earth and sky were converging to a hungry center, the philosophy of the trademark was focused to a concrete statement.

§ 2

In that deep sense which all men of all races have, in that native faculty which has come to be designated by the word "symbolism," the trademark has its origin.

By scratching pictures upon flat stones or other substances, primitive people everywhere have made their first records and communications. In time these crude drawings have invariably been simplified; and gradually certain quickly and easily made forms have come to stand for particular things, as, for instance, a circle for the sun, an upright line for a man, a curved horizontal line for a snake. And with further development certain fixed forms have come to designate particular ideas. A crossed line to the early Egyptian was an invitation to a meeting. An inverted "U" to a Sioux Indian was a challenge to a fight.

But picture-writing limited men's abilities to express themselves. And consequently we find symbols of quite another kind coming into use.

The man or men who conceived the idea of making certain marks stand for the different sounds of the human voice laid the foundation on which rests all the civilizations of the world.

The letters of our present well-ordered

alphabet are but symbols of sounds. And the words which their different arrangements form are but symbols of things or concepts.

Our common numerals are symbols in even a more direct sense. The figure four, for instance, is an arbitrary sign which by common consent has come to stand for exactly four units among all occidental nations.

Everywhere we turn this faculty of the human mind for making one thing stand for and suggest another evidences itself. Without it mental and spiritual growth would have been impossible. It separates man from the animals. It lies at the base of all progress. And with the development of human capabilities it ever gains in power.

There is a little five-pointed device which through long use has come to suggest the stars to minds everywhere. It tells the same story to the child and to his grandfather, to the Russian peasant and to the American business man.

Yet—it is not a picture of a star. It doesn't look like a star in the least. Everyone knows that stars are not five-pointed. We have always known that they are round. But we have taken this particular form as the symbol of the stars.

It is the star trademark.

And it doesn't stand for any one particular star. It is the emblem of all the stars. In a wider sense it signifies everything celestial. Also it has a religious import. It focuses a wide range of ideas.

In the same way the Christian cross has

come to have a tremendous significance. Originally it was the emblem of "the great death." Through use it came to stand for all that Christianity means. Today it is particularly the emblem of the Catholic church. With the usual sagacity which this "greatest of all business organizations" evidences in its undertakings, the symbol has been put to the best possible use. The activities of the entire system center around it. It tops every church edifice and holds the prominent place in every service. It is more heavily loaded with associations than any other symbol conceived by man.

And for this purpose no word or collection of words would have answered—for words are too complicated in form and *too definite in significance.* Only a simple form, distinct from all other forms, would have sufficed to merge so many meanings.

If we think about the matter at all we must see that symbols have multiplied in number for the reason that by their use men have been enabled to bring together and reduce to concrete forms great varieties of ideas, thereby wonderfully simplifying and strengthening their means of communication.

And we are beginning to make effective use of symbols in the business of today, for we are beginning to see that they are the simplest and most forceful means by which an association of ideas can be presented to the public mind—*and kept there.*

§ 4

In a rude hut a naked potter sat at his wheel turning into shape a pot of unusual proportions. The muddy nearby Nile flowed sluggishly under a low clay bank on which an indolent crocodile basked in the glaring sun of a day that is now ten thousand years past.

A shaggy, big muscled man was the

potter.   In his youth he had been a hunter and fisherman, and at odd times had made queer-shaped clay vessels for his own use. But one day he discovered a flat pivoted stone which he could revolve with his knees and on which he could easily mold pieces of clay into unique and accurate forms.

The vessels which he made by this new method were the envy of his neighbors, for they could not make vessels like them.

And it happened that upon a fortunate day someone offered to exchange an old pot filled with fish for one of these new creations.   Another gave a great piece of buffalo meat, and still another a measure of wild rice for the coveted vessel.

As it was more agreeable to make pots than it was to hunt and fish, pots he made, pots for others, who secured his food for him—and commerce was born.

Specialization began with a piece of clay.

This rude stone wheel was the world's first mechanical invention.

But as there were no patent laws in those dim and distant days the ingenious potter was not protected in his monopoly. After a time other pivoted stones were found. And other ambitious men, who would share his prosperity, set to work to make pots. Soon there were more pots than were needed and some of the potters had to go back to the hunt. But the inventor of the process, because of his longer experience and greater skill, still maintained himself by his wheel and continued to improve his methods and his wares.

And now he was making the greatest pot the world had yet seen. It was to be almost large enough to hold a man. And it should be the finest pot too—smooth and thin and strong and of just the right proportions. It was to be the crowning glory of his life.

But how were people to know that he had made it? He would not have it confused with the ugly unfinished things other potters were making. It was good that he should let the whole world know that he was proud of his handiwork.

And it happened that as he was finishing the vessel an inspiration came to him. He would put a mark upon its base, a mark that would distinguish it as his very own. There were no such things as signatures then. Letters had not yet been invented. But a mark a man might have, and this he would put upon all his vessels in the future as an identification, before he would let them go from his hand.

And this he did—and thus was the trademark brought into the world.

An imaginary origin, you will say. But it probably holds as much of the truth as many of the accepted tales of history.

§ 5

4000 B. C.

Chinese

The trademark is probably older than any written language. It undoubtedly had its inception in the very beginnings of trade, even before picture writing had come into use.

As it is probable that weapons were the first things manufactured by man, it is conceivable that some early genius who had the faculty of making better clubs than his fellows, and who had formed the habit of scratching his identification mark upon them, gradually began to make clubs for others, and continued the mark as evidence of his manufacture.

Or it may be that a clay molded vessel bore the first trade emblem.

This much is certain however—*trademarks were in use more than four thousand years ago.*

A recent long and careful search was rewarded by the discovery of what is probably the oldest trademark now in existence. It is an incomplete and irregular triangle— and it was stamped upon the bottom of a piece of pottery which was manufactured in Egypt more than two thousand years before Christ. A fragment of this ware is now in the British Museum.

There is a probability that marks of the kind were in use in the far east even before that far-away time. Chinese pottery of the earliest period bears a maker's or a guild's stamp which evidently was then of great antiquity.

Although the present search has painstakingly covered many fields, it may be that older emblems, which may properly be classified as trademarks, are yet to be discovered. And it may be that these will be but developments of a long and numerous series of similar emblems of still more ancient times.

§ 6

 Russian

 Adapted

In a recent year there came to us out of Russia a unique "omen of good luck" which soon came to be popularly known as the "swastika." It was an arrangement of one of the oldest symbols, probably of Aryan origin. In many different forms and at many different times it has had superstitious, religious, medical or commercial significance. Through the centuries it has experienced many "revivals"—and each revival has brought to it different or entirely new meanings.

The swastika is but one of thousands of symbols which have played a part—and sometimes a vitally important part—in the religious and secular life of all ages. Two of its forms are here shown.

The flags of the nations; the heraldic devices; the seals of government; the emblems of fraternities; all are expressions of this same spirit.

Were it possible to permanently remove every established symbol from the world we should still go our daily rounds; but the going would be slow and tedious, for our methods of communication would be clumsy and laborious.

§ 7

Symbols have occupied a more important place in the lives of the Chinese and Japanese than they ever have in ours. Things have not been so strenuously complicated over on that side of the world; there has been less hurry there and in many ways a great deal more thoroughness. The simpler life has enabled the oriental mind to comprehend many things with surprising directness and clearness.

The inability of the westerner to understand the yellow man who lives across the great sea is largely due to his ignorance of the symbols and symbolism of the east. It is part and parcel of the life there. It can't be gotten away from. And in trade the oriental has made surprisingly effective use of significant emblems.

So great has been the skill with which the trademark idea has been made to serve in Japan that large classes of men of that country are delighted to wear, as a decoration of distinction, the trademark of an exclusive maker—embroidered upon the backs of their garments.

Also, in the harmonious and attractive arrangement of commercial designs the oriental has much to teach the progressive westerner.

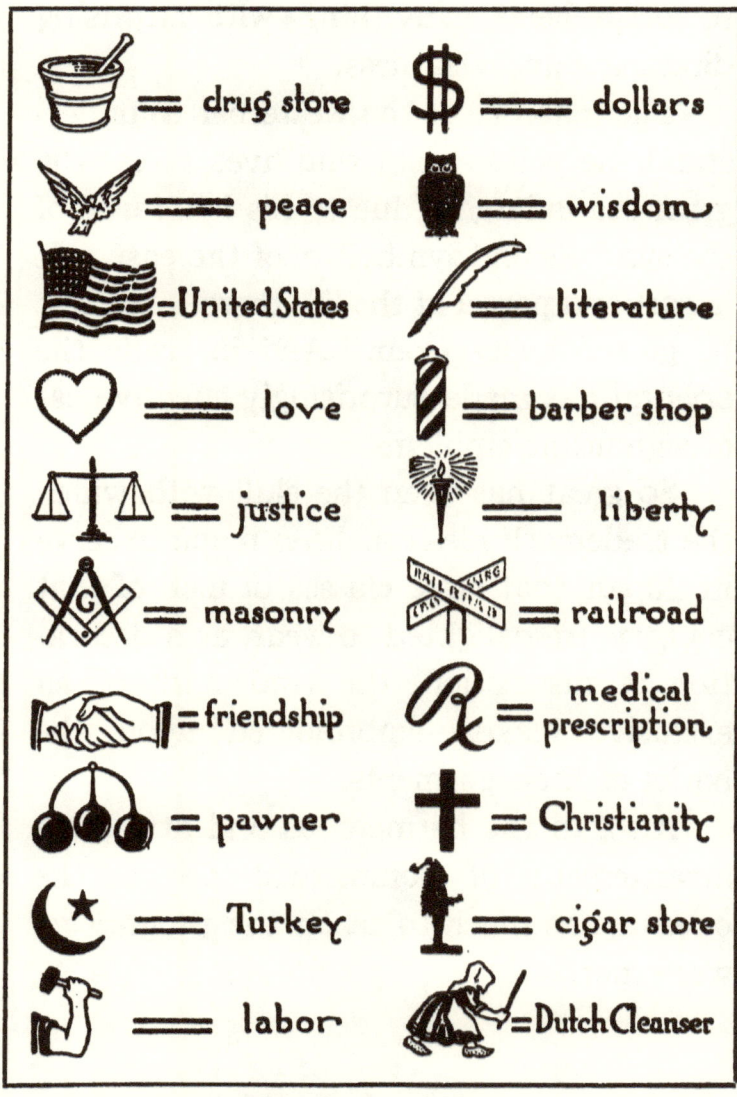

= drug store $ = dollars

= peace   = wisdom

= United States   = literature

= love   = barber shop

= justice   = liberty

= masonry   = railroad

= friendship   = medical prescription

= pawner   = Christianity

= Turkey   = cigar store

= labor   = Dutch Cleanser

SYMBOLS—THOUSANDS OF THEM SERVE IN EVERY DAY
AFFAIRS AS MEANS OF SUGGESTING "MUCH IN LITTLE"

 Celestial  Adapted

Upon a cloth of purple and gold a king paced at midnight before his tent. A great battle was to be fought, upon the issue of which hung the destinies of nations. To his new found deity the anxious king prayed fervently for a sign that would justify his faith and assure victory. At last as the dawn was breaking over the low hills the heavy clouds parted, and emblazoned upon the blue beyond, in lines of lurid fire, was a curious device made up of two ancient Greek symbols. It was the sign he had prayed for. And on that day the first Christian emperor overcame his foe Maxentius—and established in the world a new religion.

And this celestial sign the great Constantine adopted as his signet. It was his "mark of fortune." He engraved it upon his coins. It figured on his labarum and on his banners it led his hosts to battle. Where it was, there his soldiers rallied. Around it his counselors gathered. It was the symbol of the nation.

These now unbelievable tales of the supernatural origin of signs and symbols are numerous in history. But they once served the purpose of establishing the authority of the emblem. And they now serve to show how deeply the symbolizing instinct is rooted in the human consciousness.

Also to this celestial sign of Constantine's the National Biscuit Company of New York and everywhere, owes its distinctive trademark, for their well known device is an adaptation of the earlier one and has come down to us through the first published commentaries of Caesar, the books of Jenson and Elbert Hubbard's limp-leather creations.

"Sign"

Watermark

The old paper makers were probably the first manufacturers to use the trademark in its modern sense. They early discovered that by the manipulation of their screens they could produce within the paper itself permanent identification marks which would in no way interfere with the usefulness of the product. At as early a time as the fifteenth century paper makers were identifying and advertising their products by means of watermarks.

In fact some of our standard-size papers of today are called by the name of the watermarks originally used in their manufacture. A fool's cap was employed as an emblem by a maker of that size sheet. A crown marked the old "royal."

At this time Flemish and English craftsmen were also carving their "signs" upon the splendid furniture and utensils they were making. They were proud of their good work and would not part with any of it until it bore something which in effect said: *"I built this chair. It is a strong, well-made chair—and a thing of beauty as well. I did my best with it. If you want another as good, come to my shop. (Signed) John Smith."*

That was the significance of the "signs" which these master-craftsmen engraved upon their unmatched handiwork.

And manufacturers of all sorts of commodities, since that early time, have, with some degree of persistency, used trademarks upon their wares. If this has been done much as sheep follow a leader, there has been at least some vague comprehension of trademark possibilities in the doing.

And let it be remarked in passing that, as applied to the product, the trademark idea has perhaps been carried to its greatest extreme by American manufacturers of stoves. If the trademark is a good thing, they seemingly have reasoned, it is a good thing to use generously and often—and they have plastered it upon their products at every available point. The child who, of an icy morning, dresses by the family stove, is never left in doubt as to the name of the maker or the place of the making of the cheering burner that gives him friendly warmth.

§ 10

Hall-marks!

"Why, that man's character carries the stamp of the hall-mark."

What greater praise can be given one? "The hall-mark of the gentleman." True aristocracy that. It suggests tested substantiality and rare distinction. The hall-mark is the stamp of purity.

Just as Gibraltar symbolizes strength, so does the hall-mark symbolize genuineness. Both are idioms fixed in the language.

At the goldsmith's hall in London, precious metals are brought to be tested for their purity. If they measure up to a high standard, they receive the hall's stamp.

For centuries so thoroughly and honestly has this testing been done, that the stamp of the goldsmith's guild has come to signify the highest sort of genuineness throughout all English speaking countries.

When some manufacturer gives to his trademark like significance, trademark power will have developed something like hundred percent efficiency.

In a narrow frame of unfinished redwood which hangs in a clear space against a dull blue wall is a small brown print showing an open doorway in which sits a barefoot youth; beyond there appears a little garden shadowed by the high wall of an old stone house. Just as a spot of warm color the framed print has rare charm. But through the battered doorway of the picture itself ventures the imagination into the fragrance and restfulness of the inviting garden and the quaint old house—making the allurement complete. It is one of the most exquisite etchings in all the world.

Quite outside the picture and just at its lower margin is a faint and curious scroll done in pencil, which on close examination resolves itself into the semblance of a butterfly.

Yes, that it is—Whistler's butterfly. On the few choice impressions, those that he loved best, it is drawn. It did not appear on every print which he "pulled" from his amazing plates. Just those which were to his particular delight received this mark of his approval.

In this manner did the greatest of all American artists—who also manifested a peculiarly American business instinct, and was in no mean measure a pioneer advertiser of the better sort—in this manner did he make effective use of the trademark idea.

A conspicuous recognition was also given the concept in America by an artist of distinction in letters. When the brilliant and decadent Oscar Wilde lectured on this side the Atlantic he wore on the lapel of his coat a gorgeous American sunflower. He never appeared without one. He gave the flower a vogue. And something like a sensation it created. To all America it was the Wilde emblem—and it was a big factor in increasing his fame here.

These are but two of the many conspicuous expressions which *art* has given to the trademark idea.

§ 12

Thus far the point of the story is that the trademark has buried itself deep in the affairs of all races because *it is a natural and sound expression of a fundamental thing within man's inner self.*

Man has made one thing stand for and interpret an association of things and ideas and emotions since the beginning of time —and will to the end of time.

By that means he economizes his energies and makes easier the labor of his thinking. He is ever resentful toward that which requires unnecessary expenditure of energy—and he is quickly appreciative of that which minimizes such expenditures.

Symbols which have been more complicated than the idea they represent have always been rejected. Those that have long survived have been both simple and suggestive. By the elimination of the superfluities strength is gained. To reduce things to their simplest forms, that they may be with the least trouble comprehended, is the constant effort of aspiring man.

In his endeavor to find the easiest possible way for suggesting an association of ideas man invented the symbol. And as he is fundamentally economical he will ever continue to refine and amplify the symbol for the advancement of his own selfish interests.

The trademark is a means by which trade complexities are simplified. It is a means of conserving energy. And as such it is an economical factor of no small import.

The more man develops the more uses he finds for symbols.

The trademark idea is in the very life-blood of the races. And it forms a sound basis on which to build.

§ 13

Practically no manufacturer nowadays sends out his wares without some kind of an identification upon them or upon the wrappings in which they are sold. It may be that only the name and address of the maker, in ordinary letters, are placed upon them. Or it may be that a carefully thought out trademark is imprinted conspicuously upon both the merchandise and the container.

This universal practice establishes the fact that it is deemed commercially unwise for a producer to send out his wares without a means by which they may be traced back to their source.

Not alone is it the maker's pride in having made a good article that prompts him to label his wares. The consumer must identify his product. It must be protected against substitutes. And he wants re-orders. He wants to establish his product so that it will be bought by many and often. Therefore, as an evidence to the buyer that he is the responsible maker, and as an invitation for future trade, he stamps his goods with his mark.

The manner in which this marking is done is important—and it is getting to be more and more important as business advances in efficiency. If it is unthinkingly and crudely done a big and direct advantage is lost. If it is intelligently and carefully done a substantial and growing asset is gained.

§ 14

Before the development of modern advertising there were many good and apparent reasons why commodities should have been put out under well-designed trademarks.

But now, when, by these new found powers of advertising greater businesses than industry had ever dreamed of are being built up, the good and apparent reasons are multiplied by a large figure.

Under the old system the consumer came into more or less intimate contact with the producer. Now the two are usually far removed, both by distances and conditions. And the contact is established and maintained by the means of printed matter.

In the old days the package itself was practically the only bid for orders made by the manufacturer. Now he multiplies these bids a thousand fold through the public prints.

Much as a man is known by his personal appearance so is a product known by the appearance of that which stands for it in print.

Today a well advertised commodity is an old friend, while a non-advertised commodity is a stranger and has the stranger's handicap to overcome in gaining confidence.

And it is therefore immensely important that that which personifies the product to the great public should be conceived and executed so that it will perform its work with at least an adequate efficiency.

If the public eye is not given some picture that distinctly separates the product from all others of its kind nothing like adequate efficiency in this direction can be attained.

Of trademarks there are many. But there are few that measure up to the requirements placed upon them by conditions as they are today or as they will be tomorrow.

§ 15

"Willie! Willie!! Put away that book this minute. I want you to go straight to the store and get a box of crackers. And hurry too, for dinner is waiting."

Willie reluctantly dropped the latest volume of the Jack Hazard stories and with heavy feet slouched out of the door. It was a long hard trip to the grocery—almost two squares away—and the enthralling story might vanish in his absence.

From a convenient shelf the crotchety grocer handed Willie a large pasteboard box on which was pasted an ugly white label bearing the words "Sears Best Crackers." Willie knew the box well, as he knew from careful study most of the things in the grocer's stock. And, oh, how he loathed it. There was always a box of crackers to get just as Jack was about to pile a great heap of scathing scorn upon the villian's carefully pomaded head.

It was long ago that Willie made this reluctant trip to the grocery, even before the invention of the delivery system—and of modern advertising.

And — the reiteration adds the emphasis — the shelves of the shopkeepers were then practically the only advertising mediums of the producers. Their goods were displayed there, and scarcely nowhere else did "new trade" get into touch with them.

But today, by means of the printed advertisement the producer makes all the world familiar with his wares. He may if he chooses spread broadcast, pictures of his products, together with reasons why they should be bought.

But yards of cloth, boxes of crackers, matches, shoes, suits of clothing, automobiles and flying-machines all look pretty much like others of their kind, especially to the uninitiated. Pictures of the product hardly serve well the purpose of separating it from other similar products.

The manufacturer who is to be successful under the new order must do everything in his power to distinguish his goods from all goods of the kind. To make *his* stand out from the rest is one of the big problems which he has to solve.

The shopkeeper's shelves are now overcrowded with competing articles from all parts of the world. The times have changed.

Every feasible and reasonable means for giving his product distinction must be made use of by the producer who is to win in the new competition.

The old, un-distinctive white labels and the methods which gave them birth can't compete in the new order.

§ 16

The word trademark has been used to describe a multitude of things. Even in the courts of law it has been indiscriminately employed. Included within its meaning have been pictures, diagrams, initials, names, sentences, figures, faces, signatures, styles of lettering, and a wide variety of devices.

Yet the word is an excellent one. It exactly describes the function—a *mark* used in *trade*.

But not all of these things can be interpreted as marks. It will lead to clearer thinking if they are divided as follows:

1—Trade-marks
2—Trade-names
3—Trade-phrases

There is in actuality sharp distinction between these different classes. It is evidence of the rather loose thinking which has generally characterized the consideration of this important subject that the divisions were not made long ago and the lines of demarcation between them clearly drawn.

The *trademark* is a device, a unit, and has a shape independent of its lettering.

It may be a picture, a figure, or an arbitrary form containing letters.

The *trade-name* may or may not be in a distinctive style of lettering.

The *trade-phrase*, or slogan, is a pertinent expression that may appear by itself, or with the trade-name, or it may form an integral part of the trademark.

The *trade-name* is the obvious and easy expression of the idea. It follows the method that would naturally be used by the least intelligent tradesman. At best it develops but a fraction of the benefit that can be gained from the idea. But through standardization it does sometimes become a fairly efficient emblem.

The *trademark* at its best makes full use of a fundamental and vital force and is the highest expression of the idea.

If someone should ask you to let your mind dwell for a moment upon the abstract subject of lawn-mowers, you could undoubtedly bring up in your mind a fairly vivid picture of a lawn-mower as you had seen it in a hardware store or upon a lawn.

If you should then be asked to think about "Lowell lawn-mowers" not a great deal would be added to the picture. You might try to imagine what the name Lowell would look like, and wonder on what part of the tool it might appear.

But if you should be asked to think about "Keen Kutter lawn-mowers" you undoubtedly would have a more or less vivid impression of a wedge-shaped shield bearing the words "Keen Kutter" in angular letters. And by the mental picture of that device you would separate Keen Kutter lawn-mowers from all others.

The words "Snider's Catsup" may present to your mind a vivid picture of a tall bottle of thick red liquid. But the words "Jones' Catsup" would present practically the same picture.

However, it is probable that the words "Heinz Ketchup" first present to your mind a picture of a *pickle*, with a more or less vague impression that has something to do with "fifty-seven varieties." Had the pickle been presented to your mind in a more forceful manner, the association would then have been more vivid. But linked inseparably with the Heinz product is the pickle—and by that means it is distinctly separated from all like products.

Other people may have exact mental pictures of the class of things which you manufacture, but they will not separate yours from others if you give them no image to help in distinguishing it.

§ 18

The Standard Oil Company! What does it suggest to you? To your mind's eye what picture does it present?

Is it a tank car? a kerosene can? the face of the world's richest man? a striped-vested politician? the derrick of an oil well? that awful monster called "monopoly"? a Baptist church? or a bag of money?

Some picture it must present—for to think of it at all you must form some sort of mental concept of it.

The chances are that the picture which is presented to your mind by the mention of this company is a mixed, vague and uncertain thing—a sort of Cubist scramble.

But—suppose the Standard Oil Company had given you a ready-made picture or device to focus upon.

Suppose it had presented that picture or device to your eye in an attractive way a great many thousand times over a period of many years.

What then would be the result?

Surely, you would now have had a very definite and clear-cut mental picture, that would stand for and suggest to you this great institution.

And the meaning the picture would have for you would depend upon what meaning had been put into it.

Also, it is apparent that, in a large measure, that meaning would be determined and controlled by the company.

§ 19

In his last published essay Mark Twain tells of being in a great quandary. He had lost the notes of the lecture he was about to deliver. He was far from home and there was no time for rewriting them.

In desperation he took a strip of paper and drew thereon a series of simple pictures which illustrated crudely the different points of his talk in their logical order. And from this strip he delivered a lecture of two hours duration.

The plan worked so well that for future lectures he drew his crude illustrations in sequence, and then redrew them again and again, until he had them indelibly fixed in his mind.

Let Mark speak for himself. He refers to the three pictures shown here, which made the beginning of a series.

"The first one is a haystack," he says, "below it a rattlesnake—and it told me where to begin to talk ranch-life in Carson Valley.

"The second one told me where to begin to talk about a strange and violent wind that used to burst upon Carson City from the Sierra Nevadas every afternoon at two o'clock and try to blow the town away.

"The third picture as you easily perceive is lightning; its duty was to remind me when it was time to begin to talk about San Francisco weather, where there is no lightning—nor thunder either—and it never failed me."

Mark wasn't an artist, but he scratched the pictures down as best he could. And with them fixed in his mind he delivered his lengthy discourses without notes of any kind. And people marveled at his wonderful memory.

He had discovered that the mind naturally thinks in pictures—and that vivid impressions are most easily made by pictures or by picture-forms.

He had discovered the secret of the trademark idea.

§ 20

The absorbing scandal of yesterday is lost in the new sensation of today. The hurrying world easily forgets. To long keep anything conspicuously in the public mind is indeed a difficult undertaking. Remove the picture and the impression vanishes. "Out of sight out of mind." The churchmen and the political leaders have to preach the old precepts over and over again at short intervals or they would soon be remembered no more. Men and commodities of yesterday disappear today and are forgotten tomorrow. It is a changeable and fickle world.

Only those things which are constantly presented to the public mind remain there with any degree of clearness.

And the things that make the deepest impression are those which are *simplest in their arrangements* and are *brought to the attention the greatest number of times.*

One has a vivid mental concept of a spoon, for it presents few complications and is seen often. But one has only a vague idea of a complicated typesetting machine which he rarely sees.

It is easy to recall the few simple lines of "Mary had a little lamb." It is practically impossible to restate an entire Browning poem which one has read seldom and casually.

Those things which reach the attention oftenest and are freest from complications are the things that make the deepest impressions.

Let the producer try as he will, he will hardly succeed in getting implanted in the public consciousness a long and complicated series of impressions concerning any commodity, in which the public really has only an incidental interest.

As a means of focusing the general and pertinent impressions concerning a product, as a means of keeping it constantly and favorably in the public attention, the trade-mark presents surprising possibilities to the manufacturer who would build soundly and well.

§ 21

Can you reconstruct in your mind's eye a picture of the wretch who shot William McKinley? It is hardly possible. Yet undoubtedly it was vividly impressed there, for a day or two at least, and that not so very long ago.

Can you recall what a package of "Pearline" looks like? Probably not. Yet it was the most widely advertised commodity of its day and was practically the only product of its kind then in general use.

Can you form any sort of a conception of "Leviathan and Anaconda Belts" that will separate them from other kinds of belts? The chances are that you can't.

Yet these particular commodities have been called to your attention by great and costly and elaborately complicated advertisements in the very recent magazines.

Your ability to revive an image in your mind depends upon—

First—The concentration which you give to the original experience.

Second—Its freedom from complications.

Third—The number of times it is brought to your attention.

Fourth—The interest it holds for you.

Fifth—The time that elapses after it reaches your attention.

It is because the right kind of a trademark simply and economically satisfies all of these requirements as a means of making and reviving impressions that it must, with right use, become a tremendous power in commercial development.

§ 22

Suppose you were suddenly placed in a position where you would be compelled to draw from memory an exact picture of a locomotive—could you do it?

You might draw an exact picture of a telegraph pole, or even a two-story house. But in spite of the fact that you have seen thousands of locomotives, the chances are that you couldn't draw accurately a picture of one to save your life.

You may easily remember what a telegraph pole looks like—because it is simple in form. But an engine is complicated, and only a familiarity with all of its many details —a familiarity that would come from long and intimate association with it—would enable you to draw it from memory.

It is difficult enough to get even simple forms and ideas fixed in the mind. They must be forcefully presented and many times repeated if they are to leave any lasting impression there.

But it is tremendously more difficult to get complicated forms and ideas fixed in the mind. And every new complication adds to the difficulty.

A complicated trademark, like a confused advertisement, defeats the very purpose for which it is intended.

A good trademark, many times presented to the overworked public eye, must in time leave a telling impression there.

§ 23

There seems to be no limit to what some people's mouths can take in.

But there is a limit to what their eyes can hold.

Not one-tenth of one percent. of the infinite number of things that pass before your eyes today leave any impression there —any impression whatever. And only a small part of that number has held your interest. Fewer still are the things your memory will retain till tomorrow—or next year.

Present conditions put a great tax upon the eyes—and the retentive faculties. One looks at many things, but sees few. All objects of a kind are quickly and automatically assigned to their respective classes. There must be something strikingly distinctive about a street car, for instance, if it is to get particular notice.

Let it be said here again that the producer who is reaching out for public attention for his product—if he is to survive in the new competition—cannot neglect any feasible and practical means by which his product may be, in the public eye, separated from all competing products.

§ 24

In the laborious and lengthy shoptalks, tiresome descriptions and argumentative dissertations, done in uninviting arrangements of closely packed and ugly types, with which many manufacturers crowd their advertising matter, one object only is looked for.

They seek to *convince*.

But they do little or nothing to *impress*.

They put the cart before the horse— and as a consequence they get but a small part of the motive power to which they are entitled.

If one is not impressed one is not easily convinced.

Yet one may be convinced by an *impression* only. In fact, one buys a thing because he has impressions concerning it. He rarely has convictions about it.

Form has to do with the making of impressions. *Matter* has to do with the making of convictions.

If the form of the printed matter (which is the seller's ambassador to the public) is complicated, confused and uninviting, its impressiveness is nullified and its power to convince is lessened, even though the matter itself be loaded with conviction.

To *impress* as many prospective buyers as possible is the first task of those who have things for sale.

Because the trademark lends itself so well to the working out of just this purpose it becomes the logical tool for the work.

§ 25

A boy was trying to drive a short length of a square timber into hard ground.

"Why don't you sharpen it at one end?" asked a kindly gentleman. "In that way you center all the force of your pounding on one spot and the piece will go in easily."

The boy did as he was told and found

that one stroke then sent the stick further into the ground than ten had done before.

A manufacturer was trying to pound into the minds of the buying public all of the conceivable truths concerning his product. And to that end he used a great variety of illustrations and clever arguments without number—*most of which applied with equal force to competitive products.*

"But why don't you center your effort?" finally his keener-self queried. "There is only one point to every properly made stake. One can't split cordwood with a curry-comb. Put the force of your pounding on the one right spot. Center your effort and you'll find the driving easier."

Behind a carefully devised trademark he then focused his selling endeavor and thereby he at last succeeded in getting the one all-important point concerning his product driven deep into that hard and resisting substance, which for lack of a better name we call "public consciousness."

§ 26

One knows a horse by its shape. He distinguishes it from a cow, not by its colors, but by its form. There are white horses, red horses, black horses. But at a distance they are all the same shade.

Color is of secondary importance in distinguishing things.

By their shapes are objects recognized —separated from one another.

Always do we associate *forms* with *things*. We can't think of an object without thinking of its form, although we can picture it in any color we choose.

But—

On a certain table rest ten cylindrical tin cans containing soups, all of different brands, yet all practically of the same size and shape, closely resembling each other except in so far as their labels are concerned.

Down the street there pass ten automobiles, all of different makes, but to the average man as closely resembling each other as ten horses do.

There is no distinction in the shape that stands for the entire class. All objects of a kind look pretty much alike.

Distinction is best secured by associating with the individual products of the class some "different" shape that will separate it from the rest. Color alone never suffices.

To get this association established between a product and an arbitrary shape is a consummate accomplishment in merchandising.

A product is known by the trademark it keeps.

§ 27

Good wine grows in value as it grows old, but in no such marvelous proportions as a good trademark does.

The apparent thing about a good trademark is that it gains strength as it gains age.

A wise man would pay more for the Baker chocolate trademark than for all the other assets of Walter Baker & Company combined and multiplied by two.

There are any number of trademarks that could not be bought for millions. As emblems of the good-will of the business they have a tangible cash value often outranking all the other holdings of the institutions they represent.

But they did not gain their great worth in twenty-four hours. They have accumulated it. They have earned it. The power they represent today is the result of the power that has been put into them.

And be it noted that a *good* trademark accumulates power faster than a *poor* one. It would have taken Dutch Cleanser infinitely longer to have acquired the position it holds today had a letter-filled circle, or a mere name, been used instead of the sun-bonneted and symbolical figure.

What then shall we say of the manufacturer who deliberately fails to build up this asset?

Is it not likely that there will come a time when he will be looked upon as a man blind to big and apparent opportunities?

§ 28

"Oh, daddy," cried an automobilist's enthusiastic son, "we have passed four Hudsons in the last block."

"How do you know they were Hudsons, laddie?" asked the father.

"That's easy. No matter how quickly they go by I can always tell them by that funny little three cornered thing that is always on the front of the radiator. I know it because it's always in their ads too. It's a dandy little way of spotting them, daddy."

Connecting the advertising with the merchandise by means of a name alone is an ineffective way of accomplishing an important task.

It is because the trademark offers a truly scientific means of effectively linking the advertising to the merchandise that it ranks among the increasingly important factors in trade expansion.

§ 29

"Oh it's sixty-one steps from the Little Blue Hen,
To the Sign of the Pot and the Spoon,
Yet the House of the Skillet is halfway there,
Where they drink by the light o' the moon;
Hiegh-ho!
Where they dance by the light o' the moon."

Pictures talk every language. They speak the universal tongue. To the simple mind they tell their story just as they do to the cultivated intellect. People who can't read words can read pictures. The tavern and shop signs of old England guided the learned and the unlearned alike—and the children knew them unmistakably.

The well executed trademark is but a higher expression of the same idea. It talks all languages—and to all sorts of people.

§ 30

Someone will read these pages as he sits at a great desk in a busy office. It may be that it is a handsome desk, of which he is not only a little proud but also justly fond. It occupies an important place in his life. In a sense it is a part of him. It is a necessary tool in his working equipment. And quite apart from the service it renders him it may bring delight by its genuineness, its elegance of finish and design. If he thinks about the matter at all he may find that he has for it a real feeling of fellowship.

Yet, the chances are that he knows nothing of its history. He probably hasn't the slightest idea where it came from. Its origin is lost in mystery. There is no way by which he may find out who made it. Perhaps it occurs to him that he wouldn't accept a friend on the same terms. But certain it is that he would find the desk more companionable—and he would be surer of its values—if he knew all about its sources.

The consumer has the right to know who makes the things he buys.

ROUND TRADEMARKS ARE AS NUMEROUS AS CART-WHEELS AND QUITE AS LACKING IN DISTINCTION. A FEW SELECTED FROM THE MANY THOUSANDS

And what of the manufacturer who sends out his wares unidentified and unmarked? Where is the pride in his craftsmanship then? The man who shirks responsibility will shirk his work. The making of a worthy thing involves something more than the making of money. There is a question of common honesty involved here. Also a question of real business foresight.

The trademark is a moral factor.

§ 31

What the shamrock is to Ireland that the trademark is to the maker of a praiseworthy product.

It is something to arouse one's loyalty—concerning which one may have an honest emotion. Proud one may be of his native land, and tenderly he may cherish its memory. But should he not be also proud of the good work by which he lives? And does not the emblem of that worthy endeavor deserve his cherishing?

We will have better business when we have in it better balance between things of the heart and things of the head.

A good trademark is something to be loyal to.

§ 32

The question "What constitutes a good trademark?" will receive as many right answers as there are conscientious students of the subject.

One might reply by answering with the question "What makes a great play—or poem—or picture—or building—or dinner?"

An infinite number of conditions enter into the matter. And they are determined by the circumstances of each individual undertaking. To limit the work of construction by setting down any fixed rules would lead to absurdities.

There are however certain more or less obvious things which may well be avoided. Here are some of them:

First—Common and familiar forms do not usually make good trademarks, for they lack distinction. The circle, the square, the crescent, the star, the diamond, the heart, the oval, the shield, the cross, all have long ago been usurped and are burdened with significances.

Second—If one is anxious to acquire legal title to a trademark he will not have it resemble any other trademark, nor will he put in it any descriptive phrase or name.

Third—Flags and emblems of all nations, the established devices of societies, associations and institutions should be avoided as not legally usable or protectable.

Fourth—Complicated and confused pictures or devices do not make good trademarks, because they cannot be seen and comprehended at a glance. As they lack simplicity they lack strength.

Fifth—A good trademark will not depend upon any color arrangement for its effect, as it will undoubtedly be necessary to reproduce it in many places where color cannot be used.

Sixth—It is advisable to avoid designs that are higher than they are wide. A "tall" trademark is often difficult to fit into attractive and harmonious layouts.

Seventh—A trademark should be capable of reproduction by all engraving processes, by zincs, half-tones, and the different offset and lithographic methods, that it may be well printed on all kinds of paper and other printable materials.

Eighth—If the trademark is not as simple as it can be made, and carefully proportioned in all its parts, it may be found impossible to reduce it to small sizes without losing the design, or to increase it to large sizes without rendering it ugly.

Ninth—Care should be taken to evolve a design that will not print too black or too light, for undoubtedly it will be used with many styles of lettering and kinds of type faces.

Tenth—Designs that have only a temporary significance should be discarded. They may be meaningless, absurd or quite impossible of use tomorrow.

Eleventh—That which is vulgar, repulsive or ugly will never make a good trademark. Also one should be extremely cautious in the use of comic motifs.

Twelfth—It will save expense and trouble, and perhaps prevent disappointment, if the work of designing the trademark is put into trained and understanding hands. It is work that can't be hurriedly done in an idle moment by one who has no conception of the importance of the task.

A FEW GOOD TRADEMARKS, HAVING DISTINCTION AND UNITY; POSSESSING CHARACTERISTICS WHICH ENABLE THEM TO BECOME EASILY FIXED IN THE MEMORY

§ 33

"We certainly are great believers in trademarks in our company," said an executive at a recent luncheon. "We work them to the limit. We have registered more than seventy of them. Every new line we get out has a new emblem all its own. A great idea — this trademark proposition. We have never neglected it."

Yet in all the seventy there was not one trademark that had any real value —*for no particular value had been put into any one of them.* The effort of the company had been divided into seventy parts — and no one part had had force enough put behind it to make it worthy of its name.

A good trademark does not stand for a product alone. It stands for *the manufacturer and all that is behind the manufacturer and the product.* It is the emblem of all the factors that go to make the product what it is.

Could a nation have seventy flags and give to all of them worth-while significances?

It is difficult to conceive how any one company can have more than one real trademark. For if the trademark is anything it is the company's stamp of approval, its guarantee of quality, and its value depends upon how generally it is recognized as such.

Center the effort on *one* trademark and value is created; scatter it and value is dissipated.

But perhaps the chief advantage which a carefully conceived trademark brings to many companies is that it may associate and unite many styles or lines under one emblem. It brings together diversified things in a way that nothing else does. It knits together unrelated lines into a compact unit. And it wonderfully simplifies the important matter of their exploitation.

A confusion of thought leads to a multiplicity of trademarks.

KODAK

One arrangement of lines makes *a word,* that stands for an idea.

Another arrangement of lines makes *a symbol,* that stands for a product.

But words alone do not make a trademark—except by the courtesy of a lax interpretation of the term.

Letters themselves are but symbols of sounds. They are the most familiar symbols in all the world. The mind rapidly and automatically registers thousands of complicated combinations of them. In their most unique forms they present no new problem to the eye. They lack the unity and distinction which a good trademark must have.

Had it been possible for a man to have acquired legal right to the exclusive use of the letter S (or any other letter for that matter) he would have had a trademark worthy of the name.   But the letter S alone or combined with other letters, is now utterly lacking in distinction.

And words do not present unique *shapes*.

Unusual words, which have no other association, can be given trademark value. The word "Kodak" has it in large measure. But had that word also been given an unusual form, that it might have been presented to the eye as a unique design, its value certainly would have been greatly enhanced.

Unusual *lettering* may help to separate words from the common class.   But it does not carry the separation far enough.

Were it possible to make and hold a style of lettering noticeably different from all others, the measure might suffice.   But that is not possible.   Other words may be made in any distinctive style of lettering and they may be used by others.   The style cannot be protected.   And too, it is now quite impossible to originate a kind of lettering that is entirely new.

Letters in any combination or style are too common and familiar for the making of a good trademark.

§ 35

An inventor made a wonderful machine. There has never been anything like it, and it served a new human need. But in order to sell it he had to advertise it extensively. And this he did by means of a striking picture of the mechanism itself. And in time this picture served as his trademark.

But there came a day when it became necessary to redesign the machine, and in the redesigning its appearance was entirely altered. Then the trademark, which he had used so long and which to the public had come to have a definite meaning, had to be changed—and thereby was much of its accumulated value lost.

A once celebrated brand of ink came to be widely known by the peculiar texture and shape of the bottles in which it was sold. But when the price of these peculiar containers became prohibitive, they had to be discontinued, and a competitor absorbed the ruined business.

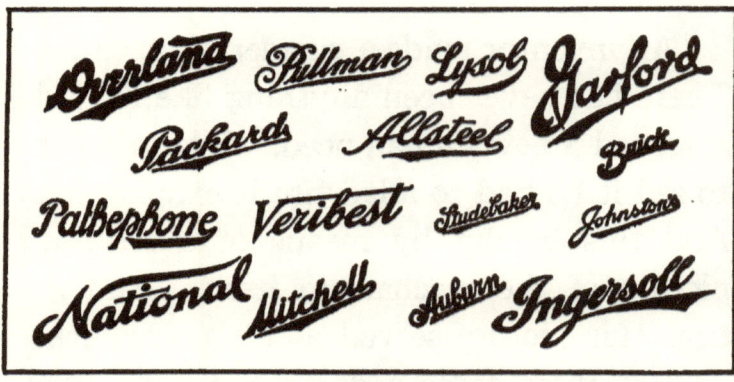

A COMMON WAY TO USE A TRADE-NAME IS TO LETTER IT IN SCRIPT AND ADD A FLOURISH. YOU WILL THEN HAVE A DEVICE THAT WILL CLOSELY RESEMBLE THOUSANDS OF OTHERS—AND THAT WILL BE SERIOUSLY LACKING IN DISTINCTION

Smith & Jones made woolens in a thriving city. By efficient management they had built up a profitable business. But on an unfortunate day Smith died and one egotistical Wilson acquired his holdings. The personality of the new man was not to be smothered, so the name was changed —and "Smith & Jones" was lost to the trade.

The picture of the automobile which a few summers ago you thought very elegant and very much up-to-date, you would scorn today as cheap and *passé.*

But the picture of the Baker Chocolate girl, who has been holding out her eternal tray to an invited public since the oldest patriarch was in swaddling clothes, undoubtedly holds an added significance for you every time she reaches your attention. She has been a familiar friend since your childhood.

Fashions and names may change, but a good trademark remains the same forever.

It sometimes happens—but not often—that a commodity itself serves well as a trademark. Ivory soap is a conspicuous example of this. But it would not be feasible for a new soap of another name to follow the identical practice. The idea has been dominated and usurped by the manufacturers of Ivory. To follow this method would be to imitate it cheaply—and unless the appearance of the competing soap were distinctly different legal difficulties would result.

And the same may be said of Royal Baking Powder.

Long use has given the names of these commodities trademark value.

Occasionally it also happens—but not often—that a package or container has trademark value. A distinct and practical shape is certainly a rare thing in containers. But Log Cabin Syrup is put up in tins that possess this advantage quite logically.

Also be it remarked here that some styles of advertising have this distinction. When a fixed style is continuously used for a long time it may acquire trademark value, providing it is decidedly unlike other advertising. The Douglas Shoe publicity—ugly as it is—is an example of this, as is also the advertising of the American Radiator Company and that which exploits Castoria.

But these successes are due to particular circumstances and to persistent and continued use. They are by no means examples to be emulated.

§ 37

The first rule for the designing of a trademark is that there are no rules. Common sense and uncommon inspiration are the best guides.

We say that a familiar form is to be avoided—especially the circle. Yet the Northern Pacific Railroad's trademark is a circle, and it is certainly one of the best trademarks that ever went on paper. Also it is one of the oldest emblems in existence. It was one of the first recognized symbols of the male and female, and is of ancient oriental origin.

The strength of this trademark, however, lies not in the circle, but in the strong and unique design that dominates it.

We say that a trademark must not be ugly. And yet the *Ostermoor* picture is a trademark in a real sense and probably could not be purchased for fortunes.

All of which gives emphasis to the truism that it's a poor rule that doesn't need fifty-seven varieties of exceptions.

§ 38

In the work of designing a trademark there are so many things to be considered that it is well to have thoroughly fixed in one's mind the advantages to be sought and the things to be avoided. To this end let us here examine a few trademarks.

But it should be borne in mind that what may be said in these pages in criticism of any trademark is said without consideration of the obstacles that may have been overcome in its development. Often defects are recognized and deplored most by those most concerned. But a trademark that has once become established can seldom be changed without serious harm. The comments here made are for the one purpose of helping to understand what a good trademark should be—and are not given in the spirit of criticism.

———

With a trade-name identical in both content and form with that of a well-known automobile, but of a much earlier origin,  the Packard Piano Company has succeeded to a remarkable degree in separating its name from the other, by this distinctive device. It is a strong trademark. It tells the story at a glance and tells it well. It is simple and is of the right proportions. It is susceptible to great enlargement and reduction without loss of its unity and it has a form that can easily be visualized. But had it held less suggestion of the shield shape it might have gained more distinction.

A square and a circle—the two commonest forms—are hardly good materials with which to build a trademark. But here is a splendid device built of them. It has all the factors demanded— simplicity — strength — difference — unity — attraction. It would probably be impossible to get this trademark registered today, as it contains a form similar to the Red Cross device. But it is the only discoverable trademark in which the square and the circle have been prominently and effectively used. Usually they should be avoided as lacking distinction.

—————

The eagle has been sadly overworked as a trademark motif—as also has the globe. But here is a combination of the two that is really impressive — principally because it produces a unit of a distinct form. It has a shape all its own. It is easy to remember — and it is symbolic.

Its great height as compared to its width is a disadvantage, as it is not so adaptable as are trademarks of less height and greater width.

A unique style of lettering may give a tradename distinction, but as the lettering **Firestone** cannot be protected, other names may be made in a similar style and the distinction thereby lost. Here is a case in point. Its peculiar **Miller** lettering has given the Firestone name some trademark value. But another rubber company has adopted a similar lettering, robbing the first of its distinction and leading to certain confusion.

Here is an example of what a trademark should not be. It is not even an adequate  protective measure. As a label it is commonplace and unattractive. Under a strict interpretation of the term it could not be classed as a trademark. With the exception of the signature it possesses no trademark value above that which cold type has.

An unusual trademark this—a happy combination of picture and design. Capable of effective use in color, or black and white. The association of the animal with the product fixes the all-necessary impression in the mind. The height of the design is a disadvantage.

This uncomplicated trademark is particularly strong because of its simplicity. It gives form to the trade-name and makes it a unit. This shape has been used for other trademarks but as the internal design is here so different and dominating, the device has the necessary distinction.

Too complicated is this elaborate emblem—and consequently too difficult to get easily fixed in the public eye. A simpler  device would accomplish this purpose quicker and with less expenditure of money and energy. And too, it is strikingly like a great many heraldic devices and may easily be confused with the Knox hat trademark, which is possessed of exceptional value because of its age and the intelligent use it has been put to.

––––––

Curiosity as to what it may be, may add interest to this strange trademark. The  end of a cypress log, badly drawn, does not make an eye-inviting picture. But it does make a fairly impressive trademark. It at least is different — and it is saved from being lost by that fact.

It has been said that a good trademark should never be round. Yet here is a round trademark that is a good one. But the circle is not essential to it. It's the emblem of someone by the name of Cross —who surely must make a worthy product. Trademarks as simple and effective as this are exceedingly rare.

There are perhaps five-hundred diamond-shaped trademarks registered in America alone. And to the great lay public they practically all look alike. Had one manufacturer been able to protect this shape, and to have everlastingly connected it with his product, he would have had a trademark of almost unmatched merit. But as there are now many different suggestions associated with the diamond, it has little or no trademark value. And the same may be said of stars, hearts, crescents and the many other familiar shapes.

―――――

A distinct shape is altogether to be desired in a trademark—but here is a distinct shape that is not particularly attractive or adaptable, and it has the disadvantage that it recalls many other associations. Also it is limiting. It might even hamper the extension of trade into foreign countries. The trademark that is not fit to be used in all places and at all times is not a good trademark.

―――――

A form totally unlike any other a trademark should have—if that is possible. But it should also have an attractive form. Here is a trademark that is "different"—but it is ugly. It is meaningless, unfinished, disjointed, and would detract from the appearance of any well laid out printing matter. Ugliness is to be avoided at any expense in the designing of trademarks.

Good nature always gives a sense of pleasure, but the comic should be employed sparingly in business. It leads to embarrassing situations—and is sometimes exceedingly cheap. One could not imagine this face being used in a Marshall Field advertisement. Yet it is a manufacturer's trademark and should properly take a place in retail advertising. Dignity adds scope to the possibilities of the trademark.

As evidence that our laws are hopelessly inadequate and that good taste is still lamentably underdone, the fact that faces are legally registerable as trademarks is here submitted. Enduring monuments to colossal egotism! It's a lenient public that forgives and forgets. Yet some faces have trademark value, and they are at least infringement proof. But in an intelligent world they are as likely to be liabilities as assets.

———

An attractive trademark this—yet as like a hundred other emblems and heraldic  devices as one pea is like another. It is dignified and inviting, but only one who had studied it closely would ever succeed in visualizing it. There have been literally hundreds of thousands of shields used since men first began to invent emblems and they are conspicuously commonplace.

———

It would seem a natural thing for an automobile manufacturer to build a radiator for his car that would have a distinct shape, and then use that shape as his trademark. The condition would be a happy one, for the conspicuousness of a distinctive radiator would quickly separate the car from all others. The good trademark of the White Company partially accomplishes this. But the shape of the radiator is hardly unusual enough. Distinction has been secured here by the addition of the other forms.

Many existing trademarks might be greatly improved by the elimination of details, or by redrawing them with a different technique. The Baker chocolate girl could be made immensely more attractive by modernizing the drawing—without affecting in any way the design or its validity. The Bell Telephone Company could have a wonderfully effective trademark by eliminating the commonplace circle and using the bell device only.

There are few trademarks that cannot be improved.

THE UNIVERSAL CAR

"Vanity on the highway" still pays a ridiculous toll for automobile travel. But two hundred thousand new Fords will this season go to buyers who prefer real service at reasonable cost rather than ostentatious display at unreasonable cost.

More than a quarter of million Fords now in service —convincing evidence of their wonderful merit. Runabout, $525; Touring Car, $600; Town Car, $800—f. o. b. Detroit, with all equipment. Get interesting "Ford Times" from Dept. F, Detroit; Ford Motor Company (insert here local branch or dealer's address in this type).

Here is one strong way to use the trademark in advertising—just one of an unlimited number of ways. But not always do conditions permit its being given the conspicuous place it held in this long series of comparatively small advertisements. This trademark is symbolic. It is made up of two old Egyptian emblems. The pyramid typifies strength, permanency, stability. The sacred ibis wings typify grace, lightness, speed. But symbolism, in this sense, is not a necessary requirement of a good trademark.

§ 39

And here follows something about the trademark as an economizing factor in *advertising.*

A large advertisement doesn't always get the most attention. A comparatively small advertisement that is unusual will sometimes secure almost maximum consideration.

Other things being equal the advertising that is harmonious in its arrangement, that has plenty of relieving white space, that is unconfused and not unnecessarily complicated, will invite most eyes.

If by the merit of a right arrangement an advertisement that occupies a quarter page is able to attract as much attention as an indifferently arranged advertisement that occupies a full page, it follows that a substantial and direct saving is made.

Large space is bought in any given publication for the purpose of attracting as many readers of that publication as possible.

If just as many readers can be impressively reached with the smaller advertisement, the saving thus made may be used in buying similar space in other publications, or in other editions of the same publication; and thereby a greater number of people are appealed to, or the same people are appealed to a greater number of times.

As a means for making effective use of small advertising space the trademark presents pertinent advantages.

We are learning that that advertising serves best which serves best as a perpetual and persisting memorandum to the prospective buyer. And into this scheme of things the trademark obtrudes itself perforce.

As an illustration of one way in which the trademark can be effectually used in small space, an advertisement of the Ford Motor Company of Detroit is printed herein. These advertisements were but two newspaper columns wide by only five inches deep, yet by their uniqueness and extreme simplicity they succeeded in dominating the page—and they accomplished more than a much greater expenditure of money had hitherto accomplished with large space.

§ 40

 Dying

 Lost

A very wise man once remarked that this old rolling world of ours would have reached its ideals long ago had the men in it not been ashamed of the finest and best things in them.

At every hand in today's business one may find unaccountable lack of courage for the carrying of the finest of purposes and beginnings to anything like their logical conclusions. It would be difficult to estimate the direct economic loss which this apparent cowardice entails.

Or perhaps it's not cowardice. It may be something infinitely more deplorable—mental stagnation.

A kindly courtesy might find excuse for the strenuous advertiser who tucks a cowardly little trademark away down in an inconspicuous corner of his advertisements, and leaves it entirely off his product.

But what shall be said of the advertiser who succeeds in building up a trademark of great and actual value, and then, for a scheme or a whim, abandons it altogether? Having put his hand to the plow he turns back.

It is use, not abuse, that gives the trademark its power. If it is worth having it is worth using with at least some degree of intelligence. Better be honest and have no trademark at all than to have one and give it no chance to perform the functions for which it was created.

The wee trademarks that are hopelessly buried in the text of advertisements and labels possess little or no worth. They are practically dead and might better be permanently buried. A victorious army carries its banner in front. Only in defeat is it trailed ignominiously behind.

A producer of a famous line of breakfast foods has recently discarded from its advertising an excellent trademark—a trademark that had taken years and the expenditure of millions of dollars to get into the public consciousness. While it never had been aggressively used, it possessed infinite value over the name printed in cold type. It was a great and tangible asset—now seemingly discarded.

And even the gutter-snipes are wondering why.

§ 41

One's title to a trademark rests in the common law. If it is originally his he may hold it, just as an author holds ownership to his unpublished manuscript. It is his by right of creation and cannot be taken away from him without his consent.

But it must be original—unlike any other. Therefore it must not infringe upon any public or private right.

It must not resemble any other trademark, or any flag, coat-of-arms, society emblem, national seal. It must be neither immoral nor scandalous. It cannot make use of an individual's name or picture without his consent, nor can it employ geographical names or terms. It must not in any way misrepresent or carry false impressions.

And since it is a trade-*mark* it must not attempt to be an advertisement, and therefore it cannot contain any descriptive matter whatsoever.

Trademarks are registered at the patent office just as a deed is registered at a county court house. But such registration does not protect it. It is merely indicative of ownership. Some valuable trademarks have never been registered. But for obvious reasons registration is always advisable.

Trademarks are protected against infringements through the courts. And therein each case rests upon its own merits. So many different constructions have been put upon the legal points involved that it is quite impossible for anyone but an expert in trademark legalities to advise concerning disputed differences. There are many lawyers who make a specialty of this phase of the law. They are not creators of trademarks. But their services are practically indispensable in the work of registration and protection.

The manufacturer who uses the care in the preparation of his trademark which other fundamentals of his business demand, will be put to no trouble for its protection and will be put to but a nominal expense for its registration.

§ 42

"We are going to change our policy concerning trademarked goods," said the head of one of the largest retail organizations in America. "From this time on we are determined to acquire and push aggressively the best and widest known brands in our lines."

"But," protested a department manager "what are to become of our own trademarked products? We certainly aren't going to —"

"That's just what we are going to do — drop them," replied the owner. "We're through putting our stamp on goods that are manufactured for us. We never have and never can control the variations in quality. Today an article may be right and tomorrow it may be all wrong—put the specifications as high as we will. We've been led into messes—"

"But surely our mark means something" argued the manager.

"It does—and in effect it's on every individual thing we sell. We stand back of our merchandise, all of it—whether it bears our trademark or not." The owner hammered his desk as he continued. "But hereafter we are going to have *two* guarantees upon all our goods—the maker's and our own. We are not going to take all of the responsibility. When things go wrong the blame isn't usually ours. But we can't shift it when our own branded stuffs are concerned. By them we have to stand or fall. If the real maker's trademark is there, it's an easy matter to adjust the trouble, without losing a customer. He sees that we are only an intermediary in the transaction. He may be 'sore'—but not entirely at us."

"You're right there!" exclaimed an assistant.

"And that's only the negative side of it," continued the owner. "We need the manufacturer's help. Why shouldn't we tap and use for ourselves some of the high voltage power he is generating by his national advertising and other propaganda? Why should we carry the entire burden? Our brands are local at best. It's easier, and a lot more profitable to travel with the current. If we can't give a woman the thing she knows about and wants, we lose her trade on other things. If we pay more for trademarked goods, we sell more of them and they sell other goods. We can't run against the established order. People want the goods they are acquainted with. We can't afford to be substituters, give-you-something-just-as-good merchants. Besides our own trademarked goods have cost us more than we think. It's at our expense that they are popularized."

"And isn't there something to be said about the right of the customer to know where his goods come from?" It was the superintendent who spoke.

"Yes, there is a question of fairness—perhaps even of common honesty—involved also," said the owner. "The customer should not be deceived as to the source of the thing he buys. And it's against public weal that the maker's identity should be lost. But enough of this. You men must think the thing through for yourself. The conference is ended."

§ 43

It is conceivable that there will come a day, and that in no far distant time, when the consumer will decree that goods that are not worthy of being trademarked will not be worthy of being bought. Fair dealing is today a recognized part of the law of the survival of the fittest. Against bad merchandise and dishonest methods the trademark is an insurance to the public—and as an insurance policy it will be demanded with the transfer of merchandise.

Others may make the goods. But others cannot use the trademark. The consumer's protection against substitution, unsatisfactory materials and bad workmanship lies in this.

And herein the trademark is an active factor in the acquirement of trade. For between trademarked and non-trademarked commodities of a kind, the educated consumer—and his number is multiplying every day—will buy that to which he can pin his faith, that which bears the maker's stamp of approval.

 Cattle brand

 Memory brand

"Whoo-pee! Whu-ya! Cut 'em in there boy! Whoo-pee! Go to it y' pink-horned piker. Wow! May your hair singe blue, y' cranky critter. Woo-boy! There y' are now. Sense ye had after all. And you're a darlin!"

A bewhiskered cowpuncher in corduroys and a derby hat, from a high seat on a Kentucky thoroughbred, sniffed the pungent odor of burning hair. All day long he had worked separating the calves from the cows, thousands of them, and now his voice was waning with the waning sun. But the job was done and the last of the calves were in the great lane—ready for the branding.

Burning! Burning deep—burning for all time—a mark never to be erased—stamped into the living flesh—seared into the very being—the cattle brand was doing its work —the young cows were being marked for life.

A brander! That's what the "trade-marker" is. His is the task of burning into the public consciousness a never-to-be-eradicated impression. His tool is hot and simple. And the depth of the burning depends upon his skill.

A brander!

§ 45

Once upon a time, not very long ago, there lived a man whose one passion in life was to bring about a condition that would compel everybody to bathe daily. The daily bath was to him the panacea for all ills. And he preached its gospel at every opportunity. In society, in business, in his letters, even in his dreams it never deserted him. His entire horizon revolved around the subject of the daily bath.

Now we know that to keep one's self clean and in shipshape is a part of common human decency. Even the truck driver recognizes that need. But the daily bath doesn't cure all evils of body and mind, any more than a good trademark rectifies all the troubles of the business.

If in these pages undue emphasis has been laid upon the importance of the trademark it has been because insufficient emphasis has been laid upon it by business in general. And it is well that the balance should be made true.

Even in advertising, the trademark is not always a vital thing. A new and unique product, which establishes a new classification, needs to be thoroughly explained and made understandable to the buyers of the field in which it sells. It would be foolhardy to try to put before the public, for instance, an automobile which operated upon an entirely new principle, by means of a trademark alone.

But there will come a time, when the new product is established and when there are many competing and similar products, when the trademark will become vitally important as a means of separating that product from all others of its kind.

The new manufacturer who does not bring into being a good trademark at the time his venture is launched, even though it may not at once be conspicuously used, is neglecting a real opportunity to add to his tangible assets.

And the established manufacturer who has not now a good trademark stands in pressing need of one.

The trademark is not a panacea for every business ill. But it is a fundamentally important part of the business equipment that is to serve efficiently in the new order.